Tasty Marijuana Laced Recipes

Edible Delicacies Laced with Ganja

Ava Archer

License

Table of Contents

Introduction

Well, to the world of cannabis in cooking. This is a mature cookbook and not meant for the fainthearted.

Marijuana has countless healing and feels good qualities and if you feel taking it via smoking is not for you, no worries.

We have rounded up 30 incredibly delicious recipes to excite your taste buds but satisfy you too. Are you ready to get high or for great food?

Canna-Crab Cake

Are you feeling moody and need a recipe to lift your mood? Try this with a little Sour Diesel to relax and calm you.

Cook time 30 minutes

Serves 4

Ingredients

- 1 egg + 1 egg yolk
- 4 tbsp mayo
- 1 tbsp yellow mustard
- 1 tbsp Sour Diesel (CBD)
- ½ tbsp Italian spice mix
- 2 tbsp butter and 2 tbsp olive oil
- ¼ cup breadcrumbs
- 1 tsp green chili chopped
- 2 cannabis leaves finely chopped
- 550g crab meat chunks
- 2 tbsp coconut flour
- Salt and pepper
- 2 tbsp water

Method

Beat the egg, mayo, mustard, CDB, spices, and chili in a bowl.

Add the coconut flour and fold in the crab meat season well and allow it to chili for better handling.

Make patties and set them aside.

Beat the egg yolk with 2 tbsp water and brush over the patties.

Coat in crumb and fry in the butter oil mix.

Serve with sprinkle cannabis leaves.

Canna-infused Green Sauce with Oyster Bake

Let the taste of the sea shine through in this delicate canna dish, and your friends will ask for me.

Cook time 10 minutes

Grill temp 145°F

Serves 4

Ingredients

- 2 dozen fresh oysters shocked
- 2 cup canna-infused green sauce
- 2 cup buttery panko crumb
- 1 tbsp chopped scallions
- Lemon wedges

Method

Heat the grill.

On a baking tray, arrange the oysters in their shells and add a tbsp of the green sauce.

Sprinkle one handful of the buttery panko crumbs over it.

Place on the grill for 30 seconds to a minute.

Serve with lemon wedges.

Ganja Pie Crust

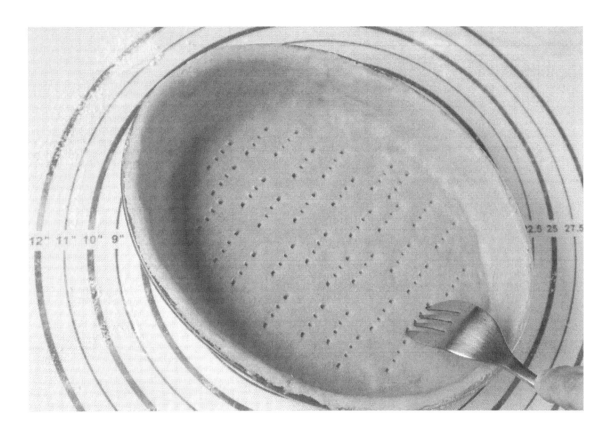

If you love pies and want to ramp the dough flavor and taste, hit it with some CBD.

Prep time – 35 minutes

Makes 9-inch pan size

Ingredients

- 1 ¼ cup AFP
- ¼ cup granddaddy purple weeds
- ¼ cup shortening
- ¼ cup unsalted butter
- 1/3 cup cold water
- ¼ tsp salt

Method

Melt the butter with water in a saucepan and the weed for 15 minutes on low.

Chill the butter mix to solidify. Remove the butter and the water for the crust.

In a bowl of flour and salt, crumble the butter and add water to bring the mix together.

Roll the dough and refrigerate it for later use.

Ginger Spiced Cannabis Brown Butter

Butter can be tasteless, but this version should make breakfast a meal to look forward to.

Prep time 60 minutes

Makes a jar

Ingredients

- 2 sticks of unsalted butter
- 1 tbsp ginger minced
- 2g CBD dried leaves
- 2 cups of water

Method

Melt the butter and ginger in a pan and keep stirring until it starts to brown.

Reduce the heat and add the CBD with a cup of water.

Simmer for 15 to 20 minutes but do not boil.

Strain the mix, freeze and then remove the frozen butter to a mixer.

Whip for 5 to 8 minutes until soft like butter.

Store in a jar and enjoy.

Marijuana Green Sauce

Soak up the benefits of CBD in your favorite sauce, and this is an amazing way to spice your favorite food.

Cook time 5 minutes

Makes a jar

Ingredients

- 2 cups basil
- ½ cup cannabis leaves
- 1 cup chives
- 4 cloves of garlic
- ½ cup sour cream
- ½ cup parsley
- Salt & black pepper
- 1 tbsp lime juice
- 2/3 cups canna oil

Method

Blend all the ingredients except the sour cream and lime juice in a blender.

Add the cream and season to taste.

Enjoy with chicken, fish, or seafood.

Blackened- Canna Dry Spice Rub

Enhance the flavor of chicken and fish with this spice rub and never look back.

Prep time 5 minutes

Makes 1 jar

Ingredients

- 2 tbsp smoked paprika
- 1 tbsp Italian Oregano
- 1 tsp salt
- 1tbsp garlic powder
- ½ tbsp onion powder
- 2 tsp cayenne
- 1 tsp chili flakes
- 1 tbsp freshly ground pepper
- 2 tbsp dried cannabis
- ½ tbsp sugar

Method

Whizz all the ingredients together in a blender until smooth as desired.

Pour in a jar and store for fish and chicken.

Cannabis-Infused Oil

If you are incorporating cannabis into your diet, you might infuse your cooking oil, as it saves you all the time doing it each time.

Cook time 6 – 8 hours

Makes 2 liters

Ingredients

- 2 liters of olive or coconut oil
- 2 cup ground cannabis (all the plant or just the flower or seeds)
- ½ bulb garlic (garlic is healthy too)

Method

In a slow cooker, add all the ingredients and allow to simmer for 6 hours or more.

This allows the potent nutrients in cannabis to sip out.

Cool it to room temperature and strain.

Bottle the oil and use it any time you want to cook.

Asian Flavored Canna-Infused Mayo

Mayo is a staple in many homes and is used as an additive in many dishes. This recipe is straightforward.

Prep time 15 minutes

Makes a jar

Ingredients

- 1 whole egg
- 2 tbsp Dijon mustard
- 1 tbsp tamarind paste
- ½ tsp chili flakes
- ¼ tsp smoked paprika
- 5 tbsp canna-oil
- ¼ sea salt

Method

Add all the ingredients into the food processor and gently drizzle the oil until an emulsion is formed.

It should be stable, thick, and creamy.

Canna-Coconut Almond Milk

Vegans will love the delicious taste of this recipe. It is simple to use Baba Kush, enabling you to sleep well at night.

Cook time 8 hours to overnight

Makes 1000ml

Ingredients

- 4 – 5g Baba Kush Cannabis
- 2 large coconut about 2 – 3 cups
- 2 cups almond
- 1-liter water

Method

Soak the coconut and almond in water overnight.

Ground the cannabis and set it aside.

Ground the coconut and almond until smooth.

Add the paste to the pot with the ground cannabis and 1 liter of water.

Cook on the low for 6 to 8 hours.

Drain over a cheesecloth, chili, bottle, and enjoy.

Citrus Canna-Sugar

We had to add this recipe here because we use sugar in sweet or savory.

Cook time 160 minutes

Oven Temp 390°F

Makes 1 jar

Ingredients

- 2 cups white sugar
- 1 cup cannabis tincture
- ½ cup lime zest
- ½ cup lime juice

Method

Preheat the oven.

Mix the ingredients in a bowl and pour on a baking sheet.

Place in the oven and leave the door ajar.

Stirring, constantly until dried.

Store and use when needed.

Coconut Cannabis Pancake

Well, breakfast is an excellent way to start the day, and being alert is a must. This recipe is a delicious way to start the day.

Cook time 20 minutes

Serves 4

Ingredients

- 1 cup cannabis whole wheat flour
- 1 cup coconut flour
- 2 tbsp sugar
- 2 tsp baking powder
- 1/3 cup shredded coconut sweetened
- 2 cup cannabis-infused coconut-almond milk
- 2 tbsp cannabis-infused coconut oil
- 2 eggs
- 1 tsp vanilla

Method

Separate the egg whites and yolks.

Add the sugar, coconut oil, and vanilla to the egg yolks and whisk until fluffy and creamier

Stir in the milk, then the dry ingredients (flour and baking powder) with coconut shred.

Beat the egg whites until soft peaks are formed.

Carefully fold the egg white into the flour batter until it is light.

In a non-stick pan, scoop a batter and cook until done.

Repeat until the batter is finished.

Serve as desired.

Herby Spicy Pot-Stada

Now you can enjoy the crisp and crunch like a Mexican restaurant. This recipe is so easy you will make it every day.

Oven Temp 390°F

Baking time 15 minutes

Serves 6

Ingredients

- 6 corn tortillas
- 2 tbsp canna oil
- 1 tsp chili powder
- 1 tsp cayenne pepper
- ½ tsp cumin
- ½ ginger powder
- 1 tsp fresh oregano chiffonade
- Salt

Method

Preheat the oven.

Arrange the tortilla on the baking tray.

Mix the oil with the rest of the ingredients.

Brush over the tortilla and bake until crisp.

Serve as desired.

Healthy Marijuana Energy Bar

For this recipe, we are using the cannabis strain Maui Wowie. It makes you relaxed, creative and reduces fatigue while keeping you alert and focused.

Prep time 20 minutes

Makes 6 – 8 bars

Ingredients

- 1 ¾ cup rolled oats
- ½ cup dried raisin
- 1 ½ cup Medjool dates pitted
- 4g of grounded Maui Wowie strain cannabis
- ½ cup semi-sweet chocolate chips
- ¾ cup honey
- 1 tsp cannabis-infused oil
- ½ cup coconut flakes
- 1 tsp ginger powder

Method

Melt the chocolate chips over a double boiler with the cannabis strain and the oil.

Keep stirring until it's smooth and silky.

Blend the honey and dates and fold them into the chocolate-cannabis sauce.

Add the ginger, coconut flakes, raisin, and oats.

Use your hands to mix well.

Scoop on a parchment-lined tray and freeze.

Cut to bars when it is set.

Cannabis Garlicky Buttered Shrimps

We are not planning to get high, but cannabis taste incredible with shrimp, and this recipe is for mature people.

Cook time 20 minutes

Serves 4

Ingredients

- 3 cannabis leaves chiffonade
- 1 cup cannabutter
- 500g fresh shrimps deveined and separated from the head and cleaned
- 2 tsp garlic minced
- 1 green chili chopped
- Salt and black pepper
- ¼ cup stock of choice
- ½ a lemon

Method

Add the butter and chiffonade cannabis to the mix.

Add the garlic, chili, salt, and pepper to it.

Add the shrimps with the head (the head is flavor).

Add the stock and replace the lid and cook on low for 2 – 4 minutes.

Remove from heat and add the lemon juice.

Serve.

Canna-Infused Corn Fritters

Treat your cannabis-loving guests to this incredible breakfast fritter with a sauce to match.

Cook time 30 minutes

Serves 4

Ingredients

- 1 tbsp cannabis chopped
- 4 cups sweet corn
- 1 red and green bell pepper chopped
- 1 red chili chopped
- 1 small onion chopped
- 1 tsp garlic minced
- 2 eggs
- 2 tbsp cannabutter
- Salt and pepper
- 1 cup breadcrumbs

Method

Partially whizz the corn in the blender and pour it into a bowl.

Add the rest of the ingredients except the butter.

Allow it to chill in the refrigerator to firm up.

Add the butter to a pan, scoop a spoonful of the batter into it to cook.

Flip and cook until set.

Serve.

Cheesy Cannabis Breakfast Muffins

Breakfast is the first meal of the day and must be fulfilling and satisfying enough and provides enough energy until lunchtime.

Cook time 25 minutes

Baking Temp – 400°F

Makes 12 muffins

Ingredients

- 1 tbsp canna oil
- 300g shredded potatoes
- 7 large eggs
- 2 tbsp fresh cannabis leaves thinly chopped
- 1 cup bacon crumbles
- 2 cups shredded cheese
- ½ mixed chopped bell pepper
- 1 tbsp scallions
- 1 small sweet onion chopped
- Salt and black pepper

Method

Preheat the oven and use the oil to brush the muffin pan.

Mix the shredded potatoes and half the cheese in a bowl and use this mix to layer the bottom of the muffin tin.

Next, beat the eggs, add the cannabis, scallion, onion, bell pepper, and season with salt and pepper.

Pour the mix halfway into the muffin tin, add bacon, fill the top, and add cheese

Repeat for all and bake for 10 minutes or until set.

Serve.

Canna Veggie Nuoc Cham

We are putting a cannabis twist to this classic Vietnamese sauce. Its sweetness and spice are the perfect balance for fried food.

Prep time 10 minutes

Makes up to 1 cup

Ingredients

- 3 tbsp cannabis sugar
- ¾ cup fresh lime juice
- ¼ cup fish sauce
- ½ cup carrot strips
- 1 bird eyes chili
- 1 green chili
- 4 cloves of garlic chopped

Method

Whisk the sugar, lime juice, fish sauce, and chilies in a bowl.

Add the rest of the ingredients and refrigerate until ready for use.

Cannabis Breakfast Smoothies

Smoothies are nutrient-packed meals for breakfast, and with the healing powers of cannabis, you cannot get it wrong.

Prep time 10 minutes

Serves 2

Ingredients

- 1 tbsp chia seed
- 1 cup coconut milk
- 200g spinach
- 2g cannabis
- 1 large banana
- 1 cup Greek yogurt
- 1 tbsp toasted pumpkin seed
- ½ bunch parsley
- 6 ice cubes

Method

Place all the ingredients in a blender and whizz away.

Pour into glasses and enjoy your day.

Marijuana Veggie Stuffed Sweet Potato Balls

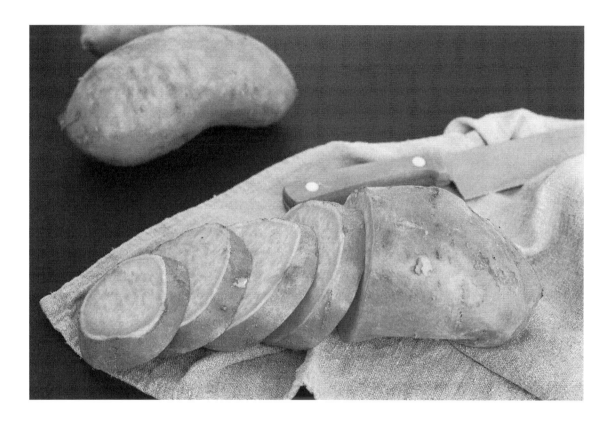

Give that potato balls some earthiness with cannabis leaves. It will certainly be a surprise for your friends or guests.

Cook time 40 minutes

Serves 4

Ingredients

- 6 cup cooked mash sweet potatoes
- 500g ground beef
- 2g ground cannabis
- ¼ cup chopped onion
- 1 tsp garlic
- 4 cannabis leaves chopped
- 12 mozzarella cheese cubes
- Salt and pepper
- 1 tbsp olive oil
- 2 eggs beaten
- 2 cup fine breadcrumbs
- Oil for frying

Method

Add the beef, ground cannabis, and chopped cannabis in a pan and cook until it turns brown.

Add the oil, garlic, and onion, then season to taste.

Allow the liquid to evaporate completely but not dried out.

Add salt and pepper to the potatoes.

Scoop a bit in your palm, flatten it out, add a cube of mozzarella and a spoon of the beef mix.

Form into a ball and dip in the egg bowl, then the breadcrumbs.

Fry on med heat until golden brown.

Canna-Mixed Berries Jam

Let the sugar be calm with this CBD-infused berries jam.

Cook time 30 -60 minutes

Makes a large jar

Ingredients

- 350g fresh strawberries
- 150g raspberries
- 170g blueberries
- 130g blackberries
- 200g brown sugar
- 4g ground cannabis
- ½ a lemon about 2tbsp juice

Method

Rinse the berries in cold water under a running tap.

Add them to the slow cooker, add the sugar and cannabis.

Cook on low heat until the juices are released.

Add the lemon juice and cook for 30 to 1 hour, occasionally stirring until it is thick.

Keep cooking until the desired thickness is attained.

Cool a bit and store in a clean jar.

Grass Herb Strawberry Sorbet

It is simple and will not take up your time. It is the perfect summer drink for a mature party.

Prep time 5 minutes

Serves 6

Ingredient

- 300g frozen strawberries
- 6 large fresh strawberries
- 8 cannabis leaves
- 1 tbsp canna sugar

Method

Whizz all the ingredients in the blender.

Pour in a freezer-safe bowl.

Canna-Infused Dry Spice Blackened Pan-Seared Fish

This delicious fish recipe is flavor-packed with incredible spice to heighten your taste buds to a new level.

Cook time – 20 minutes

Serves 4

Ingredients

- 4 large cod or salmon fillets
- 1 tsp smoked paprika
- 1 tsp ground CBD
- ½ tsp onion, garlic, and thyme powder
- ½ chili flakes
- 1 tsp black pepper
- 2 tbsp canna-oil
- 1 tsp salt
- 4 tbsp fresh parsley chopped

Method

Ground the spices together – paprika, CBD, onion, garlic, thyme, black pepper, chili flakes, and 1 tsp of sea salt together.

Arrange the fillets on a plate and dust them with the spice mix on both sides.

Add the oil to the pan and cook the fillets for 3-5 minutes on each side.

Garnish with parsley.

Serve.

It's Weed for Breakfast

A little spice never hurt, and this breakfast is a good start.

Cook time 35 minutes

Serves 2

Ingredients

- 2 eggs
- 6 rations turkey bacon
- Salt and pepper
- 2 slices white bread
- 1 large tomato sliced
- 2-3 tbsp canna-oil

Method

Add a tbsp of oil to the pan and sauté the bacon until crisp.

Set aside and add more oil if needed, crack the eggs into and cook, sunny side up.

Remove and add the tomato slices with a bit of salt and pepper.

When done, set aside and toast the slices of bread in the same pan.

Serve.

Pot Grilled Beef Tenderloin

Pampered with the perfect dry rub, this beef tenderloin combines taste, flavor, and a bit of cannabis.

Cook time 20 – 30 minutes

Grill Temp 500°F

Serves 6

Ingredients

- 1kg beef tenderloin fresh cut
- ¼ cup canna sugar
- 1 ancho chili
- ½ tbsp chili flakes
- 1 tsp kosher salt
- 2 tbsp canna oil

Method

Grind the dry ingredients and pour them into a small bowl.

Mix with the oil and use a kitchen string to tie the tenderloin to enable uniform cooking.

Apply the spice mix all over and place on the grill, and cover to cook.

Grill to required doneness.

Serve with a sauce of your choice.

Grass Potato Creamy Salad

It is healthy, tasty and you would go for a second serving.

Cook time 90 minutes

Serves 4

Ingredients

- 4 cups russet potatoes
- ¼ cup canna-infused mayo
- ¼ cup sour cream
- ½ cup chopped celery
- ½ cup chopped onion
- 1 cup chopped mixed bell pepper
- ½ tsp smoked paprika
- 1 green chili chopped
- Salt and pepper
- 2 stalks of green onion chopped
- 2 tbsp canna oil

Method

Take the potatoes chunks, season with salt and pepper, and toss in ½ tbsp oil.

Microwave them until soft.

Meanwhile, add 1 tbsp oil to the pan, sauté the celery, onion, bell peppers with the chili, paprika, and salt & pepper.

Mix the mayo and sour cream in a bowl; the potatoes should be soft by now.

Add it to a bowl, pour the sauté veggies and add the creamy mix.

Stir and sprinkle the green onions over it.

Serve.

Pot Breakfast Biscuits

We just want to make breakfast taste better and different. This biscuit recipe is flaky, canna-buttery, and tasty.

Bake Temp 400°F

Bake time 20 minutes

Makes 8 large or 10 medium

Ingredients

- 2 ¾ cups APF
- 2 ¾ tsp of baking powder
- ½ tsp sea salt
- 2 tbsp sugar
- 116g canna-butter cold and cut into cubes
- 200g canna-infused buttermilk cold
- 1 whole eggs + 1 egg yolk
- 2 tbsp cream

Method

Sift the flour, salt, sugar, baking powder in a bowl.

Add the cannabutter and mix with a potato masher to get a crumbling texture.

Add the buttermilk and eggs to form a rough dough.

Pour the dough to a dusted surface, gather it together and cut with a cutter.

Arrange on a lined tray and brush with the cream.

Bake until fluffy and brown.

Serve with cannabutter.

Cannabis Minty Mango Salsa

A kick to the regular salsa to have a party in your mouth

Prep time 10 minutes

Makes a bowl

Ingredients

- 4 cups of mangoes ripe, diced
- 1 red bell pepper diced
- 1 green bell pepper diced
- ¼ cups freshly cut cannabis leaves
- ½ bunch of cilantro chopped
- 1 tbsp lime zest
- 1 lime juiced
- 1 jalapeno deseeded chopped
- 1 tsp canna sugar
- Salt and black pepper

Method

Add everything to a bowl and squeeze the lime juice over.

Toss and refrigerate.

Serve with some crunchy tacos.

Pot-Fried Plantains

Plantain is a delicious treat that should be enjoyed with pot.

Cook time 30 minutes

Serves 2

Ingredients

- 2 ripe partially ripe plantains
- Salt and pepper
- Canna-oil for frying

Method

Peel and cut plantains into 1-inch thick round.

Fry in the oil until soft, then remove and squash with a glass.

Heat the oil more and add the flattened plantains to crisp up.

Remove, sprinkle with salt and pepper.

Serve.

Cannabis Flavored Popsicles

Ramp up the flavor in your regular Popsicle with this recipe, and it is simply delicious.

Prep time 10 minutes

Freeze time 6 – 8 hours

Makes 12 popsicles

Ingredients

- 4 cups of mango flesh
- 3 cups of blueberry
- 5 cups yogurt
- ½ cup mango juice
- ½ cup blueberry juice
- ½ cup canna sugar
- 6 cannabis leaves

Method

Blend the mango flesh, half of the yogurt, ¼ cup sugar, and 3 cannabis leaves until smooth.

Repeat the above process with the blueberries and the remaining ingredients.

Pour into Popsicle container and freeze.

When it is partially set, insert the stick and allow it to freeze well.

Marijuana Chimichurri Sauce

There is nothing like a simple sauce with all the right ingredients. Even better is with a bit of cannabis.

Prep time 5 minutes

Serves 4

Ingredients

- 1 tbsp Mexican dried oregano
- ¼ cup red wine vinegar
- ½ cup canna oil
- 1 tsp chili flakes
- 2 red chilies 4 cloves garlic
- 1 purple onion
- Sea salt to taste
- 1 bunch of parsley

Method

Wash the parsley and place it in a food processor.

Add the garlic, onion, and chilies.

Pour in a bowl and add the rest of the ingredients.

Season and allow it to rest in the refrigerator for 45 minutes before serving.

Conclusion

Do you know cannabis has health properties and is considered a superfood? Like any green vegetable, it has incredible nutrients, minerals, vitamins, and flavors.

This unique vegetable can be enjoyed in all forms – fresh or dried. While cannabis is a product you must understand before incorporating it into your diet, its healing benefits are enormous. Furthermore, food is the best way to mask its potent flavor and potency.

These 30 recipes are perfect to start. Remember; you can add them to any recipe but be wise.

Author's Afterthoughts

I can describe how grateful I am for buying this book. Every book purchased shows me that people are learning from my experience, my content. I become a writer because it is the best way to share my experience and skills.

You chose my book! From so many books on the market, you chose mine. This is very special to me. I am sure that you will find every content helpful and that you will learn a lot.

Don't forget to leave feedback after reading the book. Every feedback, even a small one can help me create even better e-books. I listen to my readers and I follow their instructions. I create content that they love. Most probably I will your honest feedback in my next books.

Thank you again

Yours Truly

Ava Archer

About the Author

There is no one more interested into gastronomy like Ava Archer is. The first thing that made her fall in love with food and cooking was seeing her grandmother cooking. That was the first time when she saw how can one meal be made perfect if you just do it with love. For her, love is the most important ingredient in one meal.

Trough the years she dedicated her life in traveling in different countries to learn traditional recipes. But also she made sure to learn about modern cuisine too. With a combination of both, she started an experiment with food to create unique and mouthwatering recipes.

In her books, you can find many types of recipes. Traditional, modern and her creations. But most importantly each recipe is explained carefully so that even beginners can start making recipes that everyone will love.

But he is not only focused on sharing her experience with the recipes. She is still researching and traveling so that she can always have something to share with the world.

She believes that everyone can create a masterpiece all that you need is to be willing to make even the weirdest combinations. You never know what can come out, maybe even the next worldwide famous meal.

Made in United States
Orlando, FL
09 March 2022